THE ILLUSTRATED WOMAN

Poetry

Division Street

No Map Could Show Them

Fiction

Black Car Burning

Non-fiction

A Line Above the Sky

THE ILLUSTRATED WOMAN

Helen Mort

Chatto & Windus
LONDON

1 3 5 7 9 10 8 6 4 2

Chatto & Windus, an imprint of Vintage, is part of the Penguin
Random House group of companies whose addresses can be
found at global.penguinrandomhouse.com

Penguin
Random House
UK

First published by Chatto & Windus in 2022

penguin.co.uk/vintage

A CIP catalogue record for this book is available
from the British Library

ISBN 9781784743222

Epigraph on p. vii © Natalie Diaz, reproduced by kind permission of the author; on
p. 23 © Don Paterson, reproduced by kind permission of the author.

Typeset in 11/14pt Minion Pro by Jouve (UK), Milton Keynes
Printed and bound in Great Britain by Clays Ltd, Elcograf S.p.A.

The authorised representative in the EEA is Penguin Random House Ireland,
Morrison Chambers, 32 Nassau Street, Dublin D02 YH68

Penguin Random House is committed to a sustainable future for
our business, our readers and our planet. This book is made
from Forest Stewardship Council® certified paper.

For Blue, Rosa & Sofia

'I touch her with the eyes of my skin.'
— NATALIE DIAZ

Contents

-skinned

THE ILLUSTRATED WOMAN

skin

Failsafe

Give me a cigarette
at the end of the line
in the Land of Green Ginger.

Lean towards me so
September's a tipped flame,
your body's a struck match,

let all this catch
and take, sip lager
from the day's unsteady glass

while colours fail
above the Humber Dock
then my words fail too

and I talk of finding them
the way someone might
say *finding cancer.*

Look out with me
until the sky becomes
the heat haze round a fire

and the packet image
of a woman in intensive care
is a pale girl painted by Vermeer,

her turban and the bright
risk of her stare, half-intimate,
the evening held

in her full earring,
how it might be pearl,
how it might be polished tin.

Love Poem

My love for you is like the Chesterfield canal, that first wall
with its spray-painted FUCK OFF, a gang of trees lining the bank
like hesitating divers, framed in the indifferent light, a single heron
and its tired, slow-motion flight towards the loading bay.
It's the Peugeot and the BMW exchanging stolen goods
an hour before dawn, parked where the path begins,
the secrecy of rain through the leaves at Brimington.
It's bee orchids and cuckoo spit, sunk, swollen mattresses,
a girl's reflection by the lock, the ghosts of narrow boats,
the lost dog who lives like a fox, split ear and puddled eyes,
roaming the undergrowth, finding the copse where a man
sleeps rough in his orange survival bag. It's the chairless
beer garden, the walkway that says DEATH TO UK COAL,
the ground they searched for the woman who never
came home. And my love for you is the light show
water makes beneath the Tapton bridge in summertime,
a shoal against the brickwork, shuddering, it's the crooked spire
and how it holds the sunset when you turn back towards town,
the watch you found in the long grass once,
still ticking, minute hand stuck over the hour.

Rain Twice

I. RAIN IN A HEADTORCH

drifts sideways through the beam,
slicks across a lemon moon

and makes the woods a mystery
of dog-scent, winter mulch.

Pre-dawn, when Sharrow Vale
and Psalter Lane lie down to weep

proud as a grandmother
and not your grandmother

but mine – tears that never fall,
caught by the landscape of her face,

tears a lifted hand could wipe away
and so I raise mine to the silver trees

and pause and look and run again
until I run like horizontal rain, run

with just my failing light
and this false gravity.

II. Night rain

Rain tiptoeing
on the roof
of your van
then quickening,

the way you say
I enter a room:
deer-like, tentative
then definite.

I can't stand
outside my body,
see myself
a shadow animal

against the wall
but I take
your word for it, lie
still on your chest

and find you
too beautiful
to look straight at
so I look at you

the way rain
touches the roof
a thousand times
lightly

trace your shoulder
the way drops
move down
the windowpane

and when you
turn to me, the rain
falls through
the night's thin skin

and my skin is less
than paper
so by now
I must be drowned

must be an envelope
soaked in warm water
held to the light
so you can

see right through me,
how I break
and make the world
seem solid.

Precious

Birmingham bright, sliver of the Jewellery Quarter
this ring is the ribcage of my great grandmother,

is the concrete pipes on the building site
where my gran played chicken as a child

crawling towards uncertain light. It is
my mother's open, newborn mouth.

There are three small diamonds, one for each
woman, nestled together.

I put my finger through
and I am entering their bodies, gently –

Nanny, with her midwife's heart
and hard edges, the bruises her husband left.

I touch her pain which is my grandmother's
curved spine, her stooping, certain gait,

her teenage years in the TB hospital,
back flat on a cool slab, the agony of stillness

which is my mother's pain, slow arthritic
pain, hard gallstones of pain

held in the core of her: my mum alone
facing the drop below the viaduct, cars passing

and lighting her briefly. She has taken
good care of this pain so that one day I will

inherit it, slip it on at night and wear it forever,
gleaming and slim. I cannot imagine it yet

but I will carry its coolness, the ache
of near-invisibility. I will be smiled at

only in pity, will lift my glittering hand
to wave goodbye to my son.

The ring fits perfectly, my fingers match theirs.
I might believe our bodies are circular –

we are born bright and we burn
down to the precious metal of our bones,

ashes to ashes,
flawed gold to gold.

The Illustrated Woman

For Sophie, my ink-sister

The Illustrated Woman

An inventory of the subject's skin
found that she was completely covered:
not as a map covers the terrain
but as a river covers its stones.

Yes, even the insides of her ears
even her labia, even the ridges
of her back teeth. We know this
to be impossible. It is as if

she wanted to leave no room
for anything to touch her.
She was not tall. Nor was she
broad across the shoulders.

Her mouth may have been small
but singling out her facial features
was difficult, such was the density
of the ink that joined them.

You might say she designed herself.
Amongst the most impressive
was a horse standing on its hind legs,
rearing on her back, nostrils steaming.

When he first examined her, the coroner
reports he heard a noise, as if a great tree
had fallen, a crash and then a quickening,
something not unlike the thunder of hooves.

A Well-known Beach

This study examined the approach behaviour of men
to women lying on a well-known beach.

The women were reading, (well-known)
lying flat on their stomachs

some with a tattoo prominently displayed
on their lower backs. On a well-known beach,

women were reading, (flat
on their well-known stomachs)

some with a tattoo on their lower backs,
some without. On a well-known beach

men were more likely to approach
the women with visible tattoos

not because they found them
to be more attractive but because

the women (well-known reading
on their lower backs) because

they believed the tattooed women
(the men well-known, the women lying

on their flat stomachs)
but because they believed the tattooed women

would be more likely to have sex
(well-known prominently displayed

on their lower backs)
more likely to have sex

on the first date
than their clear-skinned counterparts.

Source: Psychology Today: What People Really Think About Women With Tattoos

First

because your anger was a winter branch
and your cottage all beams out of true

because you lost it when I laughed under my breath
the time your staffie accidentally nutted you
lunging at a stick too big for her

because of the virginity you took
and never knew, the meals you cooked
with aubergine and parmesan that made me feel
I could be your age. Because you let me

undo my own buttons. Because the opportunities
were few. Because you said you wouldn't
make me choose between us
and university, then I chose

and you chose too. Because you told me
while we watched a film where
somebody was snorkelling
and didn't turn your face away
so your words were bubbles, lit blue,

because of your double bed, your body
the music I still travel through

because you were a stonechat
your voice was rock on rock
and you took me to a quarry for the view

because I sobbed with my face on the steering wheel
in moonstruck lay-bys and my grandma said
the moon was only passing through

this ink-shape levering from the hinge
of my spine, my first tattoo, was meant
to be a closing door

me turning my back
on you.

The Nurse

with her questions
about tattoos, her discreet scratch
at the crook of my arm
her careful drawing forth, her
did you have it done somewhere reputable?

and me, wide-eyed, fen-sick
miles from home, dreaming of tors each night
and stones shaped like eagles
saying quickly *it's on my back*
it's just on my back,

not knowing the difference
between where and whereabouts,
not knowing which way precisely
to look.

Tramp stamp

a.k.a slag tag, a.k.a sometimes informal, disparaging, a.k.a my first tattoo
at eighteen, a Celtic swirl on my lower back, slant, like the brand
of the cattle iron, the young steer quietening, steam a mushroom cloud.

In *Wedding Crashers*, Vince Vaughn says 'Tattoo? Might as well be a
    bullseye.'
Do I mean Vince Vaughn's character? The eye of a bull is a teak and
    burnt sienna marble
which blanches with stress, the sclera growing. Scientists have found

that painting large eyes on the backsides of cows can protect them
from lions and other predators. In modern branding practice, the
    animal
no longer has its legs tied, but is forced to run into a confined area and
    secured.

The scent of burning hair is like charcoal. I write *the cattle brands of
    Mitchell County Texas*
*are an ancient alphabet, Glagolitic wall writing I saw at Hum below The
    Assumption of Mary*
but if you are looking just above my waistband, you don't care I went to
    Croatia.

Two types of popular restraint are the cattle crush and the branding
    cradle.
Would you prefer to be squeezed or rocked towards what hurts you?
    Some cattle brands
that are pleasing to the mouth include *Crazy R, Diamond, Flying, Lazy,
    Slash.*

When I was growing up, low-rise jeans and B.S.E were trending.
By 2009, Barbie had a lower back tattoo. By 2015, a barmaid was able to
    go on TV
and cover up the words *Keep Calm And Carry On*, her favourite saying,

inked neatly above her buttocks. On ranches, a horizontal line is called a
    rail.
Antonio Porchia said *I know what I have given you, I do not know what
    you have received.*
The barmaid said she couldn't understand the peals of laughter

as she bent to restock fridges, white t-shirt riding up.
If horses are branded on their hooves, it is not permanent.
In 2015, Dr X wrote women with tramp stamps

are considered less athletic, less motivated, less honest, less generous
    and less artistic.
Soon afterwards, he found blonde waitresses get bigger tips, men are less
    likely to assist
women who tie their hair up and that he was being investigated.

I can't look at cattle brands without imagining my fingers stroking them,
    without touching
the raised outline of my first tattoo. If you wanted, you might ask who
    held me steady
and who made the mark? You might be curious about the hands.

Recurring Dream

where the woman etched into your left thigh
stretches her limbs, extends one foot
then disembarks your leg and walks into the world
without you, holds up the traffic on West Street
sauntering between the stalling cars

or the compass on your wrist unpeels
and leaves you stranded with yourself,

and all your lettering's removed until
you are a gravestone without moss or epitaph
and mourners squint through narrowed eyes,
desperate to know what you—

Search

Where do tattoos look the best on girls?
Elegant hummingbird. Mermaid with pearls.
Why do attractive women get tattoos?
99 soft feminine designs for you to choose!
Why does my girlfriend want to get inked?
Butterfly with falling leaf. Roses in wild pink.
Can tattoos look good on females?
The tip of her tongue. The blood under her nails.

But Mostly They Do Hearts

When Danny slips out of his t-shirt on Love Island, he's mosaiced
up to his jawline – stars, skulls, a banner that could be MUM –
and the voiceover man says: *here's a lad who wears his heart
on his sleeve. He also wears his lungs on his shins and his kidneys on his
     biceps.*

In the pause for comic effect I can pull back my cuff, reveal
the 2D heart and name I keep just under it: how the plane
in the letter 'A' keeps the sloped lines standing,
the way you hold me steady, simply hold me, son.

Bearings

I got a compass on my arm,
the sun-starved underside,
to hurt into existence
that feeling you'd left,
a landscape with no means
of reading it.

Now, south is a lie
always in my wrist,
palm and fingertips.
My clavicle and heart
must pass for north.

These blue-black lines
could be your bearings: fixed
no matter how you pivoted
in white-outs on the moors
denying your house
and the best route back.

Months afterwards
when my skin had settled,
I saw you in the station
under the satsuma glow
of announcement boards,

scanning Departures
as if you could go anywhere.
The tannoy boomed,
the domed roof echoing.

I made my body point
away from you, I turned
myself into a steady line

and because I did not want it then
you touched my back
and when I walked away
you chose
to follow me.

First Tattoo by a Woman

Holly, colouring me for days in Crookes
to the tune of Action Bronson,
my pale hip rising to the needle, blood rising
to flower under her touch.

She's working round the scar I got in Ibiza,
sprinting to a lighthouse in the rain. When I fall,
I fall properly. Rocks made swatches
of my shins, gouged a memento

from my upper thigh. Then, afternoon
and the scalpel gaze of a stranger on the beach,
his kids in the shallows and him transfixed
by my weeping skin, the whip marks and bruises,

how I wanted to have something that was mine
to show him then, or shield him,
put something bright
between me and his curiosity

so we could both name it: a dozen
large blooms in grey and pink
leaves that could smother, white dot work,
the parts which are hardest to heal.

The Tattooed Lady

'It hurt something awful, but it was worth it'.
— BETTY BROADBENT, *NEW YORK TIMES*, 1939

Portrait of Betty at a beauty pageant, the wingspan
of her small black cape. Portrait of Betty lifting up her dress
to show her thighs. Portrait of the portrait of Pancho Villa
on her leg, Madonna almost smiling from her back.
Then Betty with a zebra at the circus, tight grip
on the fur tufting its neck. Betty naked,
wearing socks and sandals, seated,
with a crystal ball at stomach height.

Betty in another century, in miniature,
an outline on a younger woman's arm,
or Betty at the end, her hands steepled
in front of her, her horn rimmed
spectacles and level stare,
her last designs on us.

Dime show

I. IRENE WOODWARD

Life has draped a garland round her neck
she can't take off. Her collarbones are roses
in full bloom. She keeps a constellation
on her arm, stars falling from a full-rigged ship.

She advertises pain-reducing oil, her beaming face
beneath the banner *Punctured Purity.* They call her
Miss to make her body more respectable.
Irene was tattooed by her father. She suffered of course
but she has delightful needlework.

Outside the high top, the ringmaster
won't meet her stare. Each night
when she twirls onto the stage
they pretend it's her first time.

II. ANONYMOUS

We don't know her name
but we know her ample salary,
that she wore a red bikini
that they called her *freak*
and that she let them drink their fill of her
so that she could eat.

III. NORA HILDEBRANDT

first branded by Martin Hildebrand
sometimes billed as her husband
and sometimes as her father,

taught to say that she was kidnapped
and tattooed by Native Americans:
no group name, just exonyms
murmurs of Sitting Bull and 'his warriors'.

The *New York Times* said
her face is so hard they must have used
a hammer for the needle.

She sits quiet
imagining the men she never met
in the evening sun's steeple.

IV. OLIVE OATMAN

emigrated west on the Santa Fe Trail
with her seven-year-old sister,
met the Yavapai
then the Mojave
and stayed

until men came to claim her five years on,
found she had drawn her own lines,
marks on her chin and arms
to show who she was
in the afterlife

and so they named it torture,
kidnapping, and brought her to a place
they called home
to show her art
as battle scars.

They left her child behind.
At night she howls:
if she doesn't know the girl's ink
how will they recognise each other
on the other side?

Lou

When she joins the dots on my sternum,
makes swifts and clover flesh
I want to be a tree with my marks telling stories.

To be read like that – rings of age, endurance.
We have been skimmed over too long, searched
at airports, scanned by our wary mothers

or men who approve so much they won't
shut up about it, wanting to touch the patterns
they can't see. We have adopted

wild poses. We have chosen to surface
what's inside and wear it brightly.
If we stand together, we become stone torsos,

unknown forms, a circle, weird and steadfast
in the middle of a sun-abandoned field. We are so
unnatural. We have been here forever,

inscribed by hail and hands, improved
by the art of spiders. Lean against us now,
try to move us, see what gives first.

Creation Myth with Rotary Machine

She gloved herself
            asked *are you ready*

then she scratched the stars first
attentive   to their preferred distance.

The crescent moon was subtle line work
and the earth grey shading.

She dispensed with colour.
        saved ochre and teal,

& the streams did what skin does
as it heals
or what the wounded heart attempts
and she had to pause
to soften them.

From time   to time
she wiped her canvas down,

checking the curvature of bark
the fronds of saplings
the assenting heads of the ferns.

There were additions,
custom shapes
she had not chosen

her hands ached   clenched
she wore a head torch and blinked

she bent double
until it was red and black and raw
and there was nothing
more she could do

then she wrapped it all in clingfilm
weeping
near-perfect

and the world was already walking,
she was murmuring   take care of this now
take good care.

On Permanence

My friend says tattoos hide the natural beauty
of the naked form. We are swimming at the mill ponds.
He steps into cold water and his skin dissolves.
My friend has seen me naked three times. We do not
speak of it, whether he found me beautiful in the morning.
Pure skin, he says, *pure design*. Around him, the water
is gorgeous with stirred-up mud, silt hanging in slow clouds.
On the bank, I stare down at my legs. I love
how the peonies on my right hip include the petal
of my deepest glassy scar, how the moles that might kill me
are stamens on flowers, how my cellulite gives texture
to sketched gritstone and the swifts on my chest
are the heart in clumsy motion. I do not think I long
to be natural, pure like the floors of airports,
like a blank expression, the aftermath of the avalanche
that buried your body whole. Each night, in the bath,
my two-year-old tries to colour me with his pastel crayons,
finishing mummy's pictures. He can't leave a page
untouched, paints with his fists and feet, pencils the walls.
In water, we are all work-in-progress, disturbing the surface
of the green pond. It is always difficult to start. The stones
unbalance me, I fall to my knees like a veteran,
survivor of wars of my body's own making.
Colposcopy. Biopsy. Sertraline and stitched tears.
Let me stay here for a moment. Let me kneel
before the sky and let me be humble, untidy,
let me be decorated.

skinless

Tollaidh

On New Year's Day, we lowered ourselves
into the loch – me, sealed in a grey wetsuit,
you in swimming trunks, walking
until the water clenched your legs too tight.

I pushed out to the centre, broke
the chill mirror at its heart and when my lungs
near-stopped and I arced back for land,
you were naked on the shoreline, facing

away from me, the small-flamed heather
at your ankles, blue towel in one hand.
Even in my numb bones, dead fingertips,
I knew the weight and warmth of you,

how much I wanted you to turn around,
wanted the landscape of your body –
the way, hours earlier, we stood
on the low path, looked out towards Slioch,

not needing to be there, just breathless
and glad for the lifted curtain of the cloud,
the track winding away from us,
the off-gold light. The sight of it.

Pip

In Monachil, we walked
through trees that clung to amber globes,
the morning unambiguously bright,
as if the sun peeled off its rind.

We learned the difference between *naranja*
and bitter *naranjo* – its double leaves
loved by the Caliphs of Cordoba,
cultivated, picked and jarred for marmalade.

I placed my hand on my stomach
as if I could already feel the growth
inside me, tiny as an orange seed,
a burrowed pip, near-weightless, citrusy.

Miles on, we can't tell if my body
is good earth, if I can keep this smallness,
sweet or sharp, if I can carry it and hold it,
gently bear the unspilled light.

Alfie

What new thing can I say to you?
Nothing about the iron birch trees
and nothing about the steady hand
of the hawk that flew above me

as I walked, carrying you inside,
until I thought we were a puppet
wobbling on the green hill, she
the master, twitching silver strings.

Nothing about the tremor of my belly
at night when you kick or grasp,
the lightness of your new bones,
the growing ache of you. I can say

something about your father
who you hear and never see.
Say, for instance, that his shoulders
are bracken and warm sand

that his eyes are his father's,
that I cut his hair close in the red
kitchen, touching his ears lightly.
But my language is tired, so I give you

the silence of an open door,
or speak to you like something I heard
once in the pattern of night rain
and never learned how to repeat.

Into the rucksack

goes the toy baby, the felt placenta, the bottle of water, into the rucksack goes the bemused smile of the dad-to-be on my right, the one with bags of crisps tattooed on his calves. Now all the men are standing. Now they must take their turn to strap the rucksack to their shoulders, wear it in front of them, awkward and gangly. Now there are sniggers and mock groans. One man rubs his back. Now they are saying *I couldn't sleep like that*. Into the rucksack goes the Sharrow School evening, the dusty classroom, the laughter and breath. Into the rucksack goes someone's earnest empathy, goes the guilt I feel when I think about my own rucksack, how it is lighter than some, into the rucksack goes my privilege, my inexplicable pain. Now the men are patting their fake bellies. Now they are taking the rucksack off again.

Advent

On the first day of Christmas, they hauled you from me
with the forceps while a crimson Santa blinked outside
and made the rain new blood.

The second day, I washed with frankincense, fed you
thin gold, summoned by the high star of your cry. The third day,
milk came swaddling-pale, shepherd's flock white.

The fourth, the fifth, I wept like a child awake
past bedtime, willing the morning close.
On the sixth day, my body was a spruce tree

and you were tinsel, wound around my ribs,
my lungs, my grateful neck. Then came days
with countless nights, nights by the window

watching sleep fly over slanting roofs outside,
its reindeer legs, its glossy chariot. By the twentieth,
you slept, prone angel on my chest.

On the twenty-first, your father was the year's first snow
to me. Then came the carol of your voice, then
your hands at the door of my heart

and here we are, the twenty-fourth, your fairy-lit eyes,
pursed lips, the snowflakes of your fingertips
and all of you a gift that I will not unwrap

just hold and hold in my forgotten hands
weighing you silently,
trying to guess what you are.

Barn Owl

Smaller than I thought and cloud-coloured, silent
through the daylight sky by Bamford Edge,
sweeping from leaf-tip to fencepost.

I cannot see the texture of her feathers, bark
of her talons, only that she must be starved
to hunt so early, dart into the corrugated barn.

I do not know why I say 'she' any more than I know
how to slake her hunger. Soon my son
cries from the car like a baby bird

and my breasts prickle and milk comes,
ghostly barn-owl pale. He is dressed in down,
nested in his blue coat. I feed him

hunched in the driver's seat, the owl rests
far in the landscape of her want. The news
reports a three-year-old from New York State

has just been saved from weeks lost in the woods.
He told his mother how a winged creature watched over him
by night, built him a rustling bed of leaves.

Truth is a milky thing, a thinness through the trees.
I cannot follow it because I hold my son.
I only hope this world will feed him.

Bear

From the day you came out of me
you were bear

musky and solid
shambling through your own world.

I looked into the dens
of your eyes,

you opened the cave of your mouth
and I knew I could not

call you mine
but I was made to guard you

lumber with you
forest-shy

in my new fur,
my loose, thin skin.

*

At night, I turn into a mother grizzly,
my hands cudgels,
my voice dredged from my chest.

I suckle you and suckle you
and you whimper
for more. Before the dawn,

we will forage
right up to the boundary
of the human,

lit with homesteads and cattle farms.
I will shield you
from dogs and sawn-off shotguns,

from fear so tangible
it becomes a bullet
a scythe.

I'll hide you inside my skull
if I have to.
We will eat what we can:

picking the day's carcass
clean, licking the bare ribs
of mountains.

*

Darling –
next Spring when snow
is memory
I will be your wife again
but in winter
I've married a grizzly
whose shadow
dwarfs mine. All day,
I dig wide circles
smell of his winter fur.

44

*I pull up roots
and our cub eats them,
greedy, pawing the earth.
At night, I am
surrounded, crushed
by my love's warm bones.
When he opens his mouth
he could swallow me.*

*Darling,
do not tend the garden
or ask me
to come out in the sun
where cats prowl
suburban flowerbeds.
Do not show me
the trellis and the pond.
I have vowed to live
in the dark, dive
into the undergrowth
when I see you,
to show the pelt
of myself only
to the bitter moon
to dance
on my hind legs
for no-one.*

*

When they found the Bear Child
of Lithuania, he walked on all fours

made low sounds that were barely human.
A ten year old, speechless,

rumbling with his own language
and no memory but leaves

under his padding hands, meat
and the sour tang of berries.

When this is over and the summer
coaxes me out, will I still speak

guttural bear? For months, my voice
has been granite, snow melt,

the place where rivers
argue with rock. When I wince

into the light will it warm
or blind me?

*

Teddy – your first word.
Ted Ted Ted

and I stare with disbelief
at the stuffed, tan animal
you dangle by the leg

or clutch to your chest
inhaling your own
heavy scent.

You carry your bears
everywhere, flatten them
with love.

My old bear skin
is hanging in the wardrobe
moth-touched,

hunched with wear
moulded to my absent shape.
One day, I might drag it out

bury my head
in the blood-and-apples
smell of it.

For now
we sit tame on the sofa
your small hand in mine

your teddy next to us
the room held, miniature
in his glassy eyes.

Wild Garlic

for Alfie

By Porter Brook, you are stubborn
as water, trampling through wild garlic,
white flowers, pale scum on the surface
of the river, aftermath of force.

You make a path and this is all
you want: circling close to the banks
repeating your steps, barely taller
than the stalks and grasses.

Then it starts to belt down, roiling,
kelching, and when I think of you
it will always be like this: you are the rain
and all its causes, you arrived

from the blue and you ran
from sunlight to shadow, unstoppable,
sturdy as a tree root, determined
to take your time.

Alfie's Poem

Mummy, I have a secret for you.
Mummy, take it from my hand.
Mummy, put your secret on your lap
where I can see it

Push the button, hear the sound

Listen to the lorikeet's whistling song.
Can you hear the call of the mynah bird?
Can you hear the flamingoes in the water?
Can you hear your small heart next to mine
and the house breathing as it holds us?
Can you hear the chainsaw start, the bones
of our neighbour's eucalyptus breaking?
It's summer, high, emptied. Listen to the ground,
giddy with thirst. Listen to the dog shit
on the lawns, the murderous water boatmen
skimming the green pond. Can you hear
the roses rioting on the trellis? Can you
make a noise like a cheeky monkey? There are
sounds your book lacks names for. Can you
hear the sleepless girls in Attercliffe?
Can you hear the aspirin of the sun dissolving?
Listen to the casual racists in the family pub.
Listen to the house Shiraz I drink as if
it's something's blood. Listen to my fear,
blooming in the vase of my chest
and listen to how I water it. Can you hear
your grandfather's lost childhood? Can you hear
the suburban library shutting? The door closing?
The books still breathing? O can you hear
the budget tightening? It's almost dark.
Listen to the noisy penguins on the ice.
Listen to my late-night online purchases.
Orange lipstick. High waisted bikini briefs.
Types of plant that will never die. Listen
to your half-sister hissing to her friends at 2am.

You hang up. No you hang up. Listen
to the panic in their emojis. Can you hear
your father lighting his first cigarette?
Can you hear the foxes mating all the way
to oblivion? Their sounds are inhuman,
too human, scaling the high fences,
pressing our windowpanes. Listen
to the utter indifference of the stars.
The night is full of holes and we
grate our bodies against them.
Can you hear that, Alfie? Can you hear me
holding you, closer than my life?
Listen to 'The Trout' by Schubert.
Listen to the blackbird's chirpy song.
Listen to this waltz by Paganini.
Listen to the stage as we walk clean
off the front of it, into the audience,
the pit, the mute orchestra.

Augmentation

I. FLAT EARTH SOCIETY

Half-shadowed, sidelong
in the mirror, I am the flat earth
no-one believes in any more

a mythic landscape
before men knew better
before maps were re-drawn.

I touch the milkless place
where my breasts bloomed
and I am tilled soil,

tamped ground: nothing
grows in me, nothing
clings to my skin.

Outside, acres of night,
the sound of a car starting,
the stars like a high road

to nowhere, fiery planets
I can't see, ribbons
of moonlight and dust.

How I want to walk them,
step out of my body,
move like an astronaut

across the surface of my life –
leaden, miraculous, chest
cratered with light.

II. LETTER TO MY BREASTS

I am sorry
for the white expensive room
that smelled of peppermint
where I let a man
indifferently span you, observe
your sparseness of tissue.

His smooth fingers
had crescent nails and large cuticles.
They left no mark
did more violence
than the man who bit you
so hard he left a nipple scarred

than those who cupped you
without permission
in nightclubs and taxi queues
those who insulted you
denied you were
even there.

He held the tape measure politely.
His hands made me believe the body
could be measured, made me betray you;
you who fed my son and made me
shiver, you who let me run
for miles in winter

who let me climb
through a squeeze of gritstone
and emerge at the top
a breathless child
with the county below me,
the cold sky above.

III. Underground

After the birth, my body was ferrous with so much blood.
I tasted wrought iron, remembered the railings in Eastwood Park
how a tree grew through and bent them, left them ruined,
perfect. First, I thought I was the metal, warped with life.
Then I held my child each night and I was the tree, sap-filled,
skin puckered by weather, sprouting wide leaves, letting
my roots taste silence underground. When my boy stopped feeding
and I fell, a part of me stayed bedded in the grass.

IV. I've heard the surgeon sits you up

unconscious
to assess his handiwork, the symmetry
and fullness of your entered skin.

Your eyes fix on nothing, your hair
falls softly, beautifully. You are
held up by an assistant's hands,

heavy and perfected, your face
emptied, as if it is enough to be upright,
half-naked. As if their work here is done.

v. Flowers

In Canada, I go to hurt at the hands
of a stranger, just to the side of my heart.

I cover my breasts with kitchen towel and tape,
two white squares, two misted windows.

Prone in the leather chair, I let him
lean in gently, touch me with a needle

and pain blooms precise and endless
through my sternum, down

to where my breath is held.
All the while, his mouth keeps working:

his girlfriend's a psycho, he's going to break
somebody's hands, he was brought up

to respect women's bodies. When this is
over, he will tell me how to heal

and I will flower in black and grey, my breasts
forever holding a small bouquet,

saying *here we are, thank you for inviting us*,
saying *we're so glad we came.*

VI. Flight

I am running
down the spine
of Sheffield,
pushing my boy
in his huge buggy.
He peers out
as if he explains me,
and will protect us
from the hecklers
who spat at my heels
when I jogged
street after street
as a teenager:
you've got no tits
you've got no tits
you've got no tits
you've got no tits.
These mud-and-
birches days, I have
outrun them,
joined with the frame
and wheels,
flesh of my flesh.
I am not the arrow
but the curve
of the bow,
look at us,
look at us now,
look how fast we go.

-skinned

The Valley

*'Just trying to get likes tbh. Inspirational quotes next to tittie pics
are soooooo annoying.'*
— AUGUST AMES, 1994–2017

I. LA

It's cocktail hour in the Valley. Above the boulevards
the sky's Pornstar Martini gold, hard to stare at long,

light dripping from the roof of a white two-storey
in Chatsworth. Inside, the sound guy's eating a bagel,

the director's three espressos down, the two male leads
are naked, scrolling PornHub on their phones, trying

to get hard, while Jessica kneels, adjusts her thong,
flicks a rope of dark hair over her shoulder.

One man has a six pack. The other is skinny with barbed tattoos.
Their hands are methodical. They don't know what to choose.

Everything exists in squares: *DP. First time anal. Czech glory hole.*
One looks from the Exit light to Jessie's nipple-coloured lipstick,

the bright mouth of the camera lens. One glances from the window
of his iPhone to the window frame. Outside the land

is hardening, parched. The palm trees grope the air.
They don't know how they got so thirsty.

II. August

Even when the Camarillo storms
had cleared and left her body
motionless, suspended from a tree,
the boys behind the Walmart store
could still find August Ames online,
long face, slim thighs, her biog
in the present tense.

When the wind drops,
the dust settles with a desert calm
across the San Fernando Valley,
dried leaves and beer cans halt
in all the corners of the parking lot.
A kid's baseball cap lies abandoned.
The moon is white, stately

as a death mask. On screen,
August moans. Think of these pixels
lifted by the hurricane, swirled into new
colours, scattered into space.
Imagine they could come to rest
in the neon of a motel sign, turn
to bright motes in your eyes.

III. Saima

Picture Saima with her long legs crossed
on the leather casting couch, backlit,
her shadow overlapping with Laurent
who leans in with his arch director's smile,

unbuttoned shirt. First, he will interview her
for the camera, then he will bend her over
the corner chair. He thinks he is excavating her
but he is only a dam in her speech.

She describes her degree in anthropology,
how porn is a kind of ethnography
and he cuts her off with *can you cook?*
She nods. Her earrings glint like scales.
She remembers the tang of fish Salan.
The lights held in the dark window
are boats at sea. This is the real ocean now
and she is casting, casting, casting.

IV. SASHA GREY

A.K.A Anna Karina
A.K.A hot sauce enthusiast,
single-malt-drinking-Dean-Martin-wannabe
posting on Twitter. A.K.A notable star
of *The Girlfriend Experience*
and *Throat: A Cautionary Tale.* A.K.A
script refuser, ad-libber, so sarcastic
it hurts. A.K.A activist. A.K.A
they can dress you up the way they want,
but they can't take away your words.
A.K.A a poet from the age of ten.
A.K.A the California kid
who wanted to build a spaceship,
makes a mean salsa, still loves Halloween.
Pumpkin lanterns, cloves and cinammon, A.K.A
I'm not as fearless as I was when I was 18.

v. Porn star name

It's the name of your first pet
and your mother's maiden name.
I wrote mine on my green jotter
at school – Lucy Pound –
in the maths class where
James and Ben poked rulers
down my top and hissed
they'd seen my lookalike
on European Blue Review last night.

I thought of Lucy Pound then,
contorting herself
through each imaginary scene,
of my mother's wedding day
her lost name,
our rabbit digging a way out
of her run again and again.

Deepfake: a pornographic ekphrastic

'The deftest leave no trace: type, send, delete.'
—DON PATERSON

I. MY BLONDE GF

This is my gf, Helen. She's amazing. I love her deeply.
I want to see her used hard, abused, and broken sexually.

What's the dirtiest thing she'd do? Tell me.
There are some great ideas in my galleries!

Your profile image is me aged nineteen.
In a floor length dress stitched with pine-green stems,

pink roses. Me aged nineteen.
My smile is tentative. My face outstares the screen.

II. HOW I WANT MY BLONDE GF USED

Here I'm grinning from a frame of blue, Ibizan sky.
Here is a woman with two men between her thighs.
Here I'm on holiday, freckled and sun flecked.
Here is a man with his hands around my neck.
Here I'm pregnant with my son.
Here is a body overrun.

III. TAGS

BDSM, Rough, interracial, BBC.
Hot wife. Captions. Cheating. DP.

IV. FAKES AND CAPTIONS BY OTHER USERS

These are the warped pixels of my face,
the features I'd learned to find commonplace,

I want to see her filled in every hole!
The eyes, which we call windows to the soul.

V. HOW MY GF GOT KNOCKED UP BY HER BOSS

This is you doing your worst.
This is language reduced to words.
This is me using you hard in a poem
where I decide what's shown.
I want to see her humiliated. Whore.
I am not humiliated. I am heavy bored

like Berryman. Bored of open flesh
and women in my area available for sex.

This is the entered body of a stranger.
This is my mouth courting danger.

VI. IMAGES UPLOADED: 1007

Your lightless room. Defend. Attack.
The lit screen giving your own face back.
The tiny tap tap of your keyboard –
the claws of a puppy crossing floorboards.

VII. LAST ONLINE ONE DAY AGO

Outside it snows and snow reclaims the lawn.
Day reclaims sky. Sky reclaims dawn.
Here is Helen walking to her son's nursery.
Here is Helen on her first anniversary.
Then comes the evening talking its cue,
the sound of history forgetting you.

This is wild

/

You've never wanted to enter the earth. Caves terrify you, toothless or bared, lit by weak excuses for sunlight. You are always climbing, trying to get as far from the ground as you can. In Greenland, on the glacier, you refused your opportunity to enter the ice. You rigged the haul rope and descent rope by the moulin and watched as the men prepared. It was orchid-shaped, twelve feet wide and boundlessly deep. Crenellated sides gave way to blue smoothness, a torrent of meltwater crashing down. It had taken days to get here, roped up and tentative, each step laboured, like walking across the surface of a moon. You tested each snow bridge for collapse. And suddenly, this roaring paleness, this glittering aura. Deep ice is incomparably blue, a clench of cold. You checked your belay device. Bill pulled his hood up, prepared to lean backwards into the moulin's throat. There were only two signals, up and down. Up meant *now*. Up meant *get me the fuck out of here*. The mountains flanked you on all sides, heraldic, stippled with snow. You watched his long body become smaller, saw him scrabbling with his crampons, reaching blindly with his axe as he was lowered further down the glacier's stem. Then he was lost to water, punched with its full force. For ages, you heard nothing. You braced against the rope, wanting to feel his good weight. Then, a strange ululation. He was alive. In fact, he was singing Gene Kelly.

/

There are things you think and cannot say. Say, for instance, that the woman's body in the altered photo reminds you of a dead horse. Brutal elegance, like that framed print you have on your wall: a picture from the aftermath of Hurricane Katrina, a fawn pony stranded in a tree, rotting entanglement, its limbs becoming branches. That her skin, marbled with shadow, looks like Jamón Ibérico. In Kulusuk, southeast Greenland, you saw a man skinning a porpoise with a flensing knife, releasing it from its structure. There were ringed seals tied to the side of the breakwater. The tethered huskies snarled at you as you passed until you were sure they smelled your blood. All night they howled like wolves, deafened you with hunger.

/

This is wild. Now you are being choked. Your eyes are mica. Now you are being forced. Your body is the place where paths run out. Now you have become a misspelled story where you are always drunk and always thirsty, always opening yourself. Now you are so cold your teeth won't stop chattering. Now you are the tundra. Now you are retreating ice.

/

You never thought you would die on the mountain, not even when the stones became a river and you were carried backwards, flailing. But you thought you would die at sunset in the camp. You always went further than was necessary from the tents to piss or shit, clutching bear flares tightly in your right hand. You always hesitated for ages, trying to find the highest, bluntest, sturdiest rock, one that might work as a screen. You were on your period and the pain made you want to crawl away like a wounded cat, find invisible corners to curl up in. Expedition stories never mention bleeding. You had slept fitfully the previous night and dreamt of polar bears outside the thin canvas of the tent, patrolling the edges of the Knud Rasmussen glacier, finding highways towards the Karale. You woke often to the clamour of birds and the rolling sounds of ice shelving into the fjord. Crouching by the rock, lowering yourself towards the gneiss and furred lichen and heather, you suddenly felt that you were being watched. There was a new, breakable stillness to the air. Your hand clutched the flares. You imagined – anticipated – the cudgels of the bear's paws, the heat and musk of it, its muzzle raised to the air. You made yourself look up. It was only an arctic fox, summer fur like cinders. It paused with one foot lifted, staring straight through you, then it danced around the rocks, almost twirling, darted towards the camp in search of food scraps. You laughed into the evening air, colder and tighter than any you'd known.

/

Perhaps you have often felt yourself watched. Perhaps you were right.

/

You admit that you have used porn. When you were pregnant, you felt so ripe with life you needed to run your hands over your own body every day. Swollen. You imagined your husband half-dressed, hidden by the cloughs on Bleaklow, fucking other women, bodies tangled in bracken and fern, pressing into each other so urgently they sank into the fickle peat. This was only exciting if you could not see the women's faces, if they were turned away or shrouded or simply out of shot. You thought of yourself as a camera, lens blurred by rain. When you told your husband, he talked about the sewage farms in Lincolnshire where he went fossil hunting as a child, the relentless horizon, the fields beyond the filter beds that yielded screwed up pages from porn magazines, images used and crumpled and flushed into the toilet. He was nine. He grew up on a pig farm, learned to use a shotgun before he was strong enough to hold it straight, leaning it on his father's strong back bent double, his father having learned in his own childhood with the barrels sawn for lightness. Your husband shot rabbits and hung them, one foot threaded through the other, from the rafters of an old chicken shed, watched the pigs fighting from the chipboard walkways above the pens and waited while his father inseminated the sows with catheters sterilised on the kitchen hob and stored on a gun-rack in his parents' bedroom. All this was natural. He knows you are too in love with mystery.

/

The year you visited East Greenland, sea ice had vanished from the fjords by June, the polar bears were starving, the hunters of Kulusuk were listless and depressed. In the northwest of the country, a US military base had emerged, rising from what once was frozen solid. Ice was reluctantly giving up its secrets. You used to think of the polar regions as inert, featureless, static with cold. You were wrong. In Alaskan Athapaskan and Tlingit oral traditions, glaciers have always been characters, agents, tricksters, a sentient environment which listens and speaks, breathes and knows. That summer, you tried too hard to hear them.

/

Since the pictures, you have learned to retreat without moving a muscle. There are strangers on the school run, men in the supermarket who seem to glance at you sideways, narrow their eyes. Do they know you? Can they see through your clothes? These times you remember how a glacier deports itself. That it is upright even as it shelves, even as it falls.

/

Approaching the Knud Rasmussen glacier by boat, every-thing was foreshortened, everything close and reachable,

everything was untouchably far. You were kept awake by the bellowing of the calving face, the booms of ice, sometimes rifle-sharp, sometimes resonant canon fire. One afternoon, you watched a buttress of ice collapse into the fjord, the sudden impact wave, a dark berg cresting from the water in its wake. That night the Northern Lights were search beams. The Inuktitut on Baffin Island describe the ice now as *uggianaqtuq* – unpredictable, unknowable, making those who live beside it restless and untethered too. Just because you are untethered doesn't mean you ever belonged there, you in your tent with your single set of clothes, your shaved head, your crampons and food cache, your plane ticket for home.

/

Days after the fake images appeared, they were removed, quietly and unbidden. The screen blinked with light. You may have thought about the wind on Bleaklow, Kinder, all the high places you run to, how a page torn up and lifted on a palm might scatter, leaf-blown, settle in the crevices of millstone grit. You thought about the flush of the cistern, the swirl of water, its power, the torrent inside a moulin, the lost archives of ice.

/

The term *you* is a foreshortened glacier. Everything seems closer than it is. You must approach quietly from the fjord, cutting the boat's engine.

/

From a distance, you might think she is enjoying herself. From a distance, the mountains look as if they are on fire. From a distance you might even admire the shape of her breasts. In your house, John Grant sings *this pain is a glacier moving through you*. You put the song on repeat. *Carving out deep valleys and creating spectacular landscapes.*

/

Your husband said they took the filter-bed pictures home
with them, him and his boy-gang; hoarded, shared and pored
over them. He said the images were shit-encrusted; piss-
soaked. There was shit everywhere in those days, slurry in the
yard where he played tennis over a bale-twine net, slipping
with every shot. In the farmhouse, his mother never worried
about letting the outside get in. Mud and dogs. Pig carcasses
in the garden. What we think of as the British countryside is
shaped and managed, planned and industrial. You realise you
have always worried about the outside getting in, even when
you are immersed in it. This is not just a fear of your own
permeability, your porous skin. You didn't want to go into the
moulin because you didn't know what you might leave there.
You felt contagious.

/

Before you packed up your last base camp, you had to pick
your way around the rocky ground with a lighter, looking
for the scraps of toilet paper left by other expeditions and
burning them. It was early September and the ground was
changing colour, leaves rusting at their tips. You squatted by
boulders, finding each paper shred and setting it aflame.
Some of them were more than shreds. Some of them bore
traces of excrement. Mostly they were just limp confetti. You
remembered the swathes of pale bog-cotton at your first camp
by the Apusiajik glacier, how they were stirred by the breeze.
A group of Ukrainian fishermen had wound up further along
the fjord and one night they invited you round for a barbecue,
grilled arctic char and cans of Carlsberg. One of the men
held his smartphone out and beckoned. *Look: blondes*, he
said. Your heart was loud. He had taken hundreds of pictures

of cotton-grass, luminescent in the sun. Platinum blonde. Pearl blonde. Each picture was perfectly framed.

/

When you look at your albums of Kulusuk, the livid sunset from the promontory, sky reflected by the ice, the blue-and-red boarded houses, the singular rocks, you wonder if your gaze is pornographic. You did not photograph the tip on the edge of town, spilling crates and broken kayaks and fridges, the shop that sold guns and laptops, the beer cans resting in hollows of grass, but perhaps you wanted to. Even at the tip of the fjord, you were thinking of new words for wilderness, wondering how to write it down, what you could carry home.

/

The boat knifing through the fjord that last time, the glacier behind you. There were minke whales breaking the water, plunging and rising again, ink-fluid, but that wasn't what moved you. It was a clutch of gulls that seemed to lift clean out of the sea, unnaturally pale as if they had come straight from the tip of a berg. Little offcuts of ice. Little sparks of ice. They rose in formation, caught by white light, then they turned as one and their bodies seemed dark. It was so simple. White then black. Black then white. To describe this without words, you would turn over your hand and hold out your palm to the sky. You leaned away from the churn of the water, into the din and lurch of the boat, towards the body of your friend and you said—

/

—and it was too loud for him to hear you so you shouted it. *If I died now* – And he smiled at you as if he had heard. The wind and water caught your words and did as they wished with them. And you really meant it. But – look – you are still here.

71

Rat

At night, a rat redrafts the lower reaches
of our house, cursive across high ledges,
forcing the bright idea of its body through masonry
to trace the lines of copper pipes. A huge buck,
gnawing plastic, caches of cat food, grazing on lintels.
With slivers of wood, he stories his kind:
lives spent shy in the bellies of ships, or prone
in a laboratory, addicted to light. Mornings,
he's heard-not-seen, scrabbling up shelves, lithe
in the corner of my eye. Why do I hate him?
He is the mother of invention.
Attacked, he slips the glove of his tail
like a lover removing a t-shirt. In groups, he
becomes a mischief. In groups, I am only a sigh.
Because he aches like me, I fear him
or feign compassion, lacing the see-saw
traps he ignores with chorizo, peanut butter.
I envy his long, loping sentences below my floor,
inside our walls, covet his fairytale fame, even
the villainy, even the placed blame. Black Death.
Lassa Fever. Such articulate history. I read him
in the hollows of the outhouse, dank cellar, stating
his case in crumbs. Even his piss is eloquent. At dusk,
I open the pantry door and he charges towards it
barrelling, a ball of midnight, muscular shadow,
come to shame me with his bravery. In India,
in the north where wild bamboo grows
there is a rat flood every fifty years. *Mautam*:
a plague spilling through grain stores.
They eat until a famine settles on the land

like rain. I know rat flood is metaphor, but here
in the dark, at the foot of the stairs I reject it,
feel them plummet from the sky, a hail of fur,
the surge of life around my knees
as I wade through their shy bodies
up to my neck. When the rat moves past me
I become a figure of speech in his damp world.
Which of us is living now? We are finished
with words.

Glasgow

The rain I brought north with me,
a Yorkshire veil, the sky
like something almost-overheard

or like the petrified grey bird
inside the Kelvingrove Museum,
its neat impression of an owl,

the stuffed, beige dog that looked
as if it might still howl,
a rooted sentry on a tall, glass case,

the cheetah with its elevated
face and one raised paw. The way
we tried to move as if we'd

not been here before.
The science test we stopped to take,
to see if we were sensitive

to bitterness – a white strip,
held for seconds on the tongue.
A strangeness they said

wouldn't last for good.
Or how you couldn't taste it
and I could.

Clematis Montana

High summer. Her garden climbs
and plummets: tendrils and vines
that have outgrown direction.

Leather flower. Virgin's bower.
Traveller's joy.

The trellis is a waterfall, flecked
with cream petals
I hold my hands out to it, a cup
or an offering.

*

My mum used to catch me out: *which is heavier,*
a tonne of bricks or a tonne of feathers?

She'd laugh. *There's no difference.* Now her limbs
are tricking her. Her body was a house.
Now it's made of feathers.

Her bones know the truth of it: mortar
and down, they share so little. Rain.
The roof of our world leaking.

Her skin lets the droplets in. Her composition matters.
Soak a brick in water and see how it trickles off.

Now soak a dozen feathers and feel the cold weight of them
press your face into your pillow at night.

*

My mother in the garden, cultivating
her hundred different types of clematis.

They are known for their ingenuity,
the incomprehensible ways they climb
and wrap around the vertical.

Andromeda. Catullus. Montana.
I love their papery strength,
their astonishment,

the thousand ways
the throat can open.

*

She has always prized rarity.
Her body is pragmatic now, her pain

an advancement of science.
Once, she wanted to leave

the sum of herself to medical students
but my father could not bear it.

For us, she does not need to be useful
or flourishing. But my mother is a gardener.

She plants nothing without thought, knows
the season for everything.

*

She is a specialist in her own suffering.
What can a consultant tell her?

They cut her: she bleeds and feels no sting.
She is weak, but her joints are painless.

I am a specialist in the scalpel
of love, the spotlight of her affection.

Dawn comes surgical, makes me wrap
my coat around my own flesh, own bones.

I should watch her now. I should be silent,
busy in the operating theatre of our lives.

*

Head in the sun, feet in the shade:
their pinks and purples are seasonal
and high maintenance.

Treated well, they can survive
a quarter of a century.
They will grow in any good soil
but there are many ways
to finish them.

Clematis montana, growing
through other plants.

When the breeze moves their blooms
they turn as one, shouting blue murder
into the wind.

Lincolnshire

Big skies, measureless above the common
and the thought of you always out there somewhere

in the frosted, furrowed ground, or the silver breath
of the horses as they chase a runner down.

You in the shingle near Mablethorpe where our dogs
pulled a glass-eyed rabbit limb from limb,

in pebbles improved by water, their smoothness,
the stutter as they skim. You on a track

behind your family farm, high grasses vanishing
towards night, the semi-precious metal of twilight

or you on wide, inconsequential roads, looping
the same song, as if we had been travelling towards

each other all along. You in the booth at the toll bridge
in the blunt nails of the man who counts the change

and in the coins that pass like rain
through the window, their glint of captured sun,

nothing counted, nothing yet to be done
with this gathering light, this small fortune.

Loch Allua

'Every swim is a little death' — PHILIP HOARE

Your body yellow
when you glance back –
a naked flame, trapped
beneath the brown glass

but – yes – you move,
you almost flicker, kicking
out towards the deepest part,
blood in your wrists ticking.

Where will you go now?
You who have never known
which shore to swim for
or which rock to call your own.

Ahead of you,
the coarse hair of the trees,
the bog beyond,
the path towards the sea.

Behind you, sunlight
and the knuckled limestone,
ground brindled with moss,
the crickets' single tone.

And God, how easy
it would be to let your arms
go slack and let the water
veil your face, lean back

and into it, your mouth
slow-opening like a fish.
But even as you almost
grant yourself the wish,

you know you are at heart
a woman who must swim.
Above your head,
three swallows dive and skim

in navy uniforms,
unbuttoned from the sky.
Watch this. How close they swoop
before they're lifted high.

Dear Body

In the shower, my mum
is a Picasso drawing –

the diagonals of her crutches,
shell-scoops of her breasts,

the folded cloth of her back
and the jut of her new hip.

Close up, her skin more tanned
than mine, a dark mole

growing on her temple,
right where my grandma's is,

her elegant, arthritic hands,
garden-blunt fingernails.

I change the temperature,
lather the soap,

holding her head
the way she held mine

in the bath before I grew
into a teenager

and only loved my bones –
those fifteen years

when hating my body
meant fearing hers,

closing my eyes
to the brushstrokes of her hair,

unpainted toes
the scar I left on her stomach.

The lovely weight now
as she leans against my arm,

skin damp with steam
and together,

we inch back
towards the frame.

Acknowledgements

Poems in this collection first appeared in POETRY, the *TLS*, *Rialto*, *Extra Teeth*, *Bath Mag*, *Now Then* and *Poetry Review*. Poems from 'The Illustrated Woman' sequence were broadcast on Radio 4.

Some of these pieces started life in dialogue with Katrina Naomi and appeared in *Same But Different* (Hazel Press) – thank you Katrina for your energy, wisdom and insight.

Thanks to Parisa Ebrahimi, Clara Farmer, Charlotte Humphery, Amanda Waters, Rebecca Goss and Alan Buckley for their editorial input. Thanks also to Kate Fletcher, Rachel Bower, Kim Moore, Suzannah Evans, Andrew Forster and Sophie Sparham for writerly support and to my family, especially Jess.

An early draft of this collection won a Northern Writers' Award in 2018 – I am incredibly grateful for this support which came at a crucial time.

Thanks to Trey, Holly and Lou for the ink. You're my favourite artists.

Notes on Poems

The Illustrated Woman – For further reading on the history of women and tattoos, I recommend *Bodies of Subversion: A Secret History of Women and Tattoos* by Margot Mifflin (Powerhouse Books, 2013) and *Covered in Ink: Tattoos, Women and the Politics of the Body* by Beverly Yuen Thompson (NYU Press, 2015). If you're interested in tattoos in literature, try Dorothy Parker's *Elbow: Tattoos on Writers, Writers on Tattoos* edited by Kim Addonizio (Grand Central Publishing, 2003). The quotation by Vince Vaughn in the poem 'Tramp Stamp' is taken from *Wedding Crashers* (2005), written by Bob Fisher and Steve Faber. The Antonio Porchia reference in the same poem is taken from *Voices: Aphorisms*, selected and translated by W. S. Merwin (New York: Alfred A. Knopf, 1988).

The Valley – Poems in this sequence were loosely inspired by Jon Ronson's Podcasts 'The Butterfly Effect' and 'The Last Days of August'. These poems are fictional responses and do not represent the views of real people. In some cases names of women who work in porn have been changed to protect their privacy. The poem 'Sasha Grey' is intended as a tribute to the artist Sasha Grey. Quotes adapted from 'Sasha Grey: Music is just like the porn industry', interview with Beaumont-Thomas, www.theguardian.com, 25 October 2012. The poem 'August' is a response to the death of August Ames (born Mercedes Grabowski), who was a Canadian pornographic actress. She appeared in almost 290 movies, including a non-pornographic film in 2016, and was nominated for several AVN Awards. In 2017 at the age of 23, Ames took her own life.

Deepfake: a pornographic ekphrastic – In 2021, I discovered that someone had taken non-intimate images of me from social media sites and manipulated them to create violent porn, accompanied by threatening descriptions. At the time, this wasn't illegal under UK law. In response, I started campaigning to raise awareness around image-based abuse. If you have been affected by any similar issues, the Revenge Porn Helpline are a really useful source of information and support: https://revengepornhelpline.org.uk.

This is wild – The song lyrics in this poem come from 'Glacier', written by John Grant and Birgir Thorarinsson.

Loch Allua – The epigraph to this poem comes from *RISINGTIDEFALL-INGSTAR* by Philip Hoare (4th Estate, 2017).